立ち上がれ 目覚めよ
スワーミー・ヴィヴェーカーナンダのメッセージ

Arise Awake
Messages of Swami Vivekananda

日本ヴェーダーンタ協会
Vedanta Society of Japan

スワーミー・ヴィヴェーカーナンダ生誕150周年記念出版
A Swami Vivekananda 150th Birth Anniversary Commemoration Publication

スワーミー・ヴィヴェーカーナンダ
Swami Vivekananda

目　次
CONTENTS

出版者の言葉

スワーミー・ヴィヴェーカーナンダ ……………………… 7

メッセージ：

    力と信仰………………………………12

    愛とお世話……………………………18

    神と宗教………………………………21

    霊的な実践……………………………29

    その他…………………………………34

Publisher's Note

Swami Vivekananda ……………………………40

Messages :

    Strength and Faith……………………………45

    Love and Service ……………………………53

    God and Religion ……………………………57

    Spiritual Practice ……………………………63

    Miscellaneous……………………………66

出版者の言葉

　この本にはスワーミー・ヴィヴェーカーナンダの力強いメッセージが収められてあり、そのどれもがありきたりの人生を理想の人生に変える可能性を秘めています。これらのメッセージを学び、その魂を吸収することで、これまで世界中の多くの人々に影響を与えてきました。それは今日までも続いています。

　この本はとても小さな本ですが、読者の皆様が全くの混乱と絶望、弱さに打ちひしがれているときに、新しい希望と力を注ぎ込み、価値ある人生を生きるために大きく役立つこと心から祈願しています。

　最後にスワーミージーのメッセージは、英語の部分と日本語の部分では順序が一致していないことをお伝えしておきます。

スワーミー・ヴィヴェーカーナンダ

(1863〜1902)

立ち上がれ 目覚めよ

　スワーミー・ヴィヴェーカーナンダ（1863～1902）は、インドで生まれ、カルカッタ大学を卒業し、シュリー・ラーマクリシュナと出会いました。シュリー・ラーマクリシュナは近代インドの神人で、スワーミー・ヴィヴェーカーナンダの友人、哲学者、師となりました。後年、スワーミージーは、家庭と家を捨て、出家僧となりましたが、それは最高の真理を悟り、生涯を人類への奉仕に奉げるためでした。

　スワーミー・ヴィヴェーカーナンダは1893年、シカゴでの第一回万国宗教会議において宗教の調和を説いた演説により、西洋で著名になりました。以来、西洋とインドでヴェーダーンタ哲学と普遍主義についての講演を行い、大勢の人を啓蒙しました。マハトマ・ガンジーや詩人ラビンドラナート・タゴール、政治家ジャワハルラール・ネルー、自由のための戦士スバス・チャンドラ・ボース、タタ財閥、鉄鋼会社、自動車会社の創始者ジャムセットジ・タタをはじめ、同時代のインドの多くの偉人がスワーミー・ヴィヴェーカーナンダに影響を受けたと述べ

ています。また、スワーミーはアメリカの慈善家ジョン・D・ロックフェラーと科学者のニコラ・テスラ、ロシアの小説家レフ・トルストイ、ノーベル賞を受賞しヴィヴェーカーナンダの古典的な伝記を書いたフランスのロマン・ロランなど西洋の著名人にも影響を与えました。

　スワーミー・ヴィヴェーカーナンダは日本とも特別な関わりがあります。シカゴの宗教会議に行く途中この国に立ち寄り、1893年7月に約3週間滞在したのです。スワーミーはこの滞在中に見聞したものを称賛しています。日本国民の愛国心、勤勉、倫理観、美的センスなどに着目し、その資質が優れていると褒め称えたのです。このことは横浜から出された7月13日付の手紙に書かれています。

　著名な日本人美術史家、岡倉天心は、スワーミーの熱心な信者で客員美術学生であったジョセフィン・マックロードを通じて、スワーミー・ヴィヴェーカーナンダの著書に出会いました。天心は後日、カルカッタ近くの新しいラーマクリシュナ僧院とミッション本部を訪れ、日本を再訪し、ヒンドゥ教につ

いての講演をしてもらえるよう、スワーミー・ヴィヴェーカーナンダに懇願しました。しかし健康が悪化したため、スワーミーは再び日本の地を踏むことはできませんでした。

スワーミー・ヴィヴェーカーナンダのメッセージは今日でも当を得たものです。それは世界中の多くの著名な思想家、宗教指導者、政治家が、今なおスワーミーのメッセージからインスピレーションを受けているという事実からも分かります。

メッセージ

力と信仰

　立ち上がれ。目覚めよ。ゴールに達するまで立ちどまるな。

　アメーバの状態から人間に至るまでの自分自身の歴史を振り返ってみよ。誰がこれだけのことをしたのか？　君自身の意志がしたのだ。それなら、どうして君の意志が万能であることを否定できよう？　君たちをそれほどの高みまで昇らせることのできたものは、君たちを更にもっと高いところで行かせることができるのだ。君に必要なのは、その意志をいっそう強固なものにする性格である。

　ある人と別の人との間に天と地の開きがあるのは、その人が自分自身を信じているか、信じていないかによる、と見ることができる。自分自身を信じている人は、何でもする。私は自分の人生においてそのことを経験してきたし、現在もそうし続けている。年をとるにつれ、その信念はますます強くなっ

Arise Awake

ている。

　おんみ、地上の神々——罪びとたちよ！　人を罪びととと呼ぶことが罪なのだ。それは人間性への変ることのない名誉毀損である。さあ来たまえ、おお、ライオンたち、そして自分は羊だという迷妄を振り落したまえ。おんみたちは恵まれた、永遠の、不死の魂であり自由な霊である。おんみたちは物質ではない、おんみたちは肉体ではない。物質はおんみの召使なのである。おんみが物質の召使なのではない。

　それぞれの国に、ただ１ダースのライオンの魂をあらしめよ。かれ自身の束縛をたち切ったライオン、無限者にさわった、その全霊がブラフマンに行ったライオン、富にも力にも名声にも目をくれぬライオンである。これだけで、全世界をゆさぶるに十分であろう。

　たとえ君たちが３億３０００万の神話の神々を信仰し、また外国人が君たちの中につれてきたすべて

の神々を信じたとしても、それでもなお、君たち自身への信仰を持たぬなら、君たちにとって救いはない。君たち自身を信じ、その信仰の上に立ちあがれ。

　まず自分を、それから神を信じよ。

　もし君が5つの知識を自分のものとし、自分の人生と人格形成に活かすことができれば、図書館にあるすべての本を暗記した人よりも教養があると言える。

　宇宙のいっさいの力は本来われわれのもの。われわれは目を自分の手でふさいで暗いといって泣いている。自分のまわりに闇など存在しないことを知れ。両手を開けば、そこは元からある光に満ちている。闇は存在せず、弱さも存在しない。弱いといって泣くのは愚か者だ。清らかになれないといって泣くのは愚か者だ。

　強さは生、弱さは死、これはおおいなる事実だ。

Arise Awake

力強さは幸福であり、永遠の生であり、不滅である。弱さは不断の緊張と不幸をもたらす死だ。

　自分を信じない者は無神論者だ。古い宗教は神を信じない者を無神論者とよぶ。新しい宗教は自分を信じない者を無神論者という。

　失敗を気にするな。それは自然なことだ。失敗――それは人生の美だ。失敗のない人生などありえない。もがき苦しむことがなければ人生に意味はない。詩もなくなってしまうだろう。苦しみや間違いを気に病むな。私は牛が嘘をつくのを聞いた事がない。牛はただの牛であって、人間ではないのだ。だからこれらの失敗や小さな後退を気にするな。千回でも理想を掲げよ。そしてもし千回失敗したら、さらにもう一度チャレンジせよ。

　弱さの治療薬とは、弱さについて考えることではなく、強さについて考えることだ。人には強さについて教えよ。それは既にわれわれの中にあるのだ。

立ち上がれ 目覚めよ

　信じること、信じること、自分自身を信じること、神を信じること——これが偉大さの秘訣だ。……自分自身を信じ、自分自身への信仰に立脚して、強くあれ。

　世界の歴史は、彼ら自らを信じたごく僅かな人びとの歴史である。その信仰が、内なる神を呼び出すのだ。君たちは何でもすることができる。無限の力を現す努力を十分にしないときにのみ、失敗するのだ。人または民族がかれ自身またはそれ自身への信仰を失うや否や、死がやって来る。まず自分を、それから神を信じよ。

　世界は数百人の勇敢な男性および女性を必要としている。人生の真理を知る勇気を持ち、死を前にして恐れおののくどころか、死を喜んで受け入れ、「自分の本質は魂であり、全宇宙であり、何物も自分を殺すことはできない」ということを人に自覚させる、そのような大胆さを常に発揮せよ。

Arise Awake

　成功するためには、非常な忍耐力と強大な意志を持たなければならない。「私は大海を飲み干す」「私の意志をもってすれば、山も粉々に崩れ去る」と不屈の魂は言う。そのような強い意志を持ち、懸命に働くのだ。そうすれば、目標に到達するだろう。

　善であること、善をなすことがあらゆる信仰の要である。

　汝らは神の子。永遠の至福の自己であり、神聖で完全な存在だ。地上の神である君たちが──罪びとだって？　人をそう呼ぶことこそ罪であり、人間の本性への侮辱だ。来たれ獅子たちよ、そして自分が羊であるという妄想を振り払え。君たちは不滅の魂であり、自由な精神であり、祝福された永遠の存在なのだ。

　年を取るにつれて、私は自分がいっそう、小さいもの事の中に偉大さを探し求めるようになっている

ことに気づく。誰でもが、偉大な地位に立てば偉大である。臆病者でも、脚光を浴びていれば勇敢になる。世間が見ているのだから！ しだいにつよく、私には、真の偉大さは、あの、その時々にだまって着実にわが務めを行ないつつあるイモ虫の偉大さである、と思うのだ。

勇敢で、力強くあれ。山のような障害を克服する意志を持て。君が欲する力と救済は、君の内にある。

力は生命であり、弱さは死だ。自分を身体的に、精神的に、霊的に弱めるものは、毒のように吐き出しなさい。

愛とお世話

もし、世界の役に立ちたいと思うなら、それを非難するのはやめよ。これ以上世界を弱くするな。何が罪で、何が不幸か。罪も不幸もまさに弱さから生じたのではないか？ 世界はそのような教えによっ

て毎日ますます弱められている。

　もし君が君自身の救済を求めるなら、君は地獄に行くだろう。君が求めなければならないのは他者の救済だ。そして、もし君が他者のために働いて地獄に行かなければならないとしても、それは自分の救済をねがって天国に行くよりも価値がある。

　わが国にたとえ1匹の犬でも食べものがなくている間は、私の宗教はそれに食べさせることだ。

　愛する者は生き、利己的な者は死ぬ。だから愛のために愛しなさい。それが人生の唯一の法則なのだ。君たちが生きるために呼吸するのと同じように。これが無私の愛、無私の行為、その他の無私の付く言葉を実践する秘訣である。

　愛に失敗はないのだよ、君。今日であろうと、明日であろうと、何十年後であろうと、真実は征服する！　愛は必ず勝つ。君は仲間を愛しているか？

立ち上がれ 目覚めよ

愛の絶大な力を信じなさい……君には愛があるか？　(愛があれば)君は万能だ。君は完全に無私無欲か？　もしそうなら、君には抵抗できない。それはどこでも損をしない性格である。

自己主張ではなく、自己犠牲が最高宇宙の法則である。

祝福を数えて、問題を数えるな。愛する祖国の恵まれない兄弟姉妹のために、いかに役立てるかをつねに考えよ。

純粋であり他者に善をなすこと、それがあらゆる礼拝の要点だ。貧しい者、弱い者、病気の人びとのなかにシヴァ神を見るものが真のシヴァ神の礼拝者だ。人がもし神像のなかにしかシヴァ神を見ないなら、彼の礼拝はまだ準備段階に過ぎない。

世界中の宗教は精彩を欠いたまがいものになって

いる。世界が求めているのは個性的な人間だ。その人の人生は燃え上がる愛そのもので、私心のかけらもないような人びとを必要としている。その愛は、その人の口から発せられる一語一語を落雷のように響かせる。

他者のために生きる者だけが、本当に生きている。その他の者は生きながらにして死んでいるのだ。他者のためになされたごくわずかな仕事でさえ、獅子の力強さを心に教え込むだろう。

神と宗教

アジアの声は昔から宗教の声である。ヨーロッパの声は政治の声である。

君たちは神を探しにどこへ行こうとしているのか？ あらゆる貧しい人、不幸な人びと、弱い人びとは神ではないのか！ なぜ最初に彼らを拝まないのだ！ なぜガンガーの岸辺に井戸を堀りに

行くのか。

　インドは、もし彼女が神の探求をつづけるなら、不死である。

　この宗教は、われわれインド人がヨーガ、すなわち合一と呼ぶものによって成就される。労働者にとって、それは自分たちと人類全体の合一であり、神秘主義者にとっては自己の低俗な部分と崇高な部分の合一であり、恋人にとっては、自分自身と恋愛の神の合一であり、哲学者にとってはあらゆる存在の合一である。これが、ヨーガが意味しているものなのだ。

　この利他の精神は、宗教の判断基準である。利他の精神が勝っている人は、よりスピリチュアルであり、よりシヴァに近い。そしてもし人が利己的であるなら、どんなに多くの寺院を見ても、どんなに多くの巡礼地を訪れても、そして額に豹のような模様を塗っていても、彼はシヴァから遠く

離れているのだ。

　すべてのものを神として礼拝せよ。形あるものはすべて神の寺院である。その他はすべて妄想だ。常に内面を見つめ、決して外側のことに目を奪われるな。神とはヴェーダーンタに説かれているようなものであり、神を礼拝するということもそうである。

　すべての魂は潜在的には神聖である。目標は、内外の自然を制御して内なる神性を現すことである。このことを働き、礼拝、心の統御、または哲学によって——これらの1つ、2つ以上、または全部によって——なし、自由になれ。これが宗教の全部である。教義とか信条とか儀式とか書物、寺院等々は第二義的な些末事だ。

　すべての宗教の理想はひとつ、自由を得る事と、不幸の無くなる事である。

　もし主が慈悲深いお方でないのなら、海には1滴

立ち上がれ 目覚めよ

の水もないだろうし、深い森に1本の小枝もないだろうし、富の神の家にひとかけらのパンくずもないだろう。かれがそう思召せば、砂漠に水は流れるだろうし、乞食は山ほど持つだろう。かれは1羽のスズメの落ちるのもご覧になる。これらは単なる言葉であるか、それとも文字通りの事実であるか？

もし神が存在するなら、彼を見なければならない。もし魂があるのなら、それを知覚しなければならない。それをしないなら信じないほうがましだ。偽善者であるより率直な無神論者であるほうがよい。

恐怖があってはならない。もの乞いはいけない。要求である。最高者に要求せよ。母の本当の信者は鉄石のように堅く、ライオンのように恐れを知らない。彼らは、たとえ全宇宙がかれの足もとで突然こなごなに砕けても、いささかもあわてないのだ！ 彼女をして、君に耳を傾けさせよ。いささかでも母へのへつらいがあってはならぬ！ おぼえていたまえ、彼女は全能なのだ。石からでも英雄たちをつく

ることができるのだ！

　私が説くのは愛、愛だけであり、私の教えは、宇宙の本質の同一性と普遍性を説いている偉大なヴェーダーンタの真理に基づいている。

　私は、ヒンドゥの社会を改善するのに宗教の破壊は必要ではない、社会の現状は宗教のためにこうなったのではなく、宗教があるべき形で社会に適用されなかったためにこうなったのである、と主張する。

　私は、政治または社会の進歩は不要だなどと言っているのではない。私が言おうとしていること、そして君たちに心にとめておいて貰いたいと思っていることは、ここではそれらは二義的なもの、一番たいせつなのは宗教だ、ということである。

　私は過去のあらゆる宗教を受け入れ、それらすべての宗教とともに神を礼拝する。それらがどのよう

な形の神を礼拝していようと、あらゆる宗教といっしょになって神を礼拝する。私はイスラーム教のモスクにも行くし、キリスト教の教会へも入って十字架の前にひざまずく。仏教の寺院に入っては、ブッダと仏道に帰依する。森の中ではあらゆる人の心を啓発する光を見ようと試みているヒンドゥ教徒とともに瞑想をする。

　実在する唯一の神、私の信じる唯一の神——いっさいの霊魂の総計——を礼拝できるよう、私を幾たびも生まれ変わらせ、私に幾千の不幸をなめさせたまえ。何にもまして、あらゆる人類、種族の中におわす私の神なる悪人、私の神なる不幸な人、私の神なる貧しい人が、私の礼拝の特別な対象なのだ。

　主は、生の中にも死の中にも、幸福の中にも不幸の中にも平等に存在しておられる。全世界は主で満たされているのだ。目を開き、主を見よ。

　宗教はほんとうになにかを成就できるのか？　で

きる。それは人びとに永遠の生命をもたらす。それは人間をあるべき存在にし、動物的人間を神にする。

　宗教は教理や教義にはなく、知的な議論にもない。宗教とは、あることであり、成ることであり、悟ることである。

　宗教は形而上世界の真理を扱う、ちょうど化学その他の自然科学が自然界の真理をとり扱うように。

　宗教は真剣な自己犠牲を伴う。自分自身のためには何ひとつ望むな。あらゆることを他者のために行え。それは、自分という存在を愛し、動かして神の中に置くことである。

　神を礼拝することで、われわれはいつもわれわれ自身の隠れた真我を礼拝してきたのだ。

　人格の形成に、善い偉大なあらゆるものをつくるために、また他者および自分に平安をもたらすため

に、宗教は最高の動機力であり、したがってその立場に立って学ばれるべきだ。宗教の、せまい、限られた、闘争的な思想は、すべて、無くならなければならないのだ。宗教ではすべての宗派的観念および部族または民族の観念は、捨てられなければならない。それぞれの部族または民族が自分の神を持ち、他の神はどれも悪い、と考えるのは迷信である。「それはもう過去のもの、そのような考えは、すべて、捨てられなければならない」

　人間社会から宗教を取り去ったら何が残るか。ケモノたちの森だけである。感覚の幸福は人間の目標ではない。知恵（ギャーナ）が、すべての生命の目標である。

　人生に厳しい打撃を受け、この世の一切物に失望した時に始めて、われわれはもっと高い何ものかを欲する。その時に神を探し求めるのだ。

　人類の究極目標、すべての宗教の目的はたったひ

とつ——神との、つまり各人の本性であるところの神性との、再結合である。

世界中にあるさまざまな宗教は、それぞれが行っている礼拝の形式に違いはあるが、本当はひとつなのだ。

世俗の仕事というものはない。すべての仕事は宗教であり礼拝である。

霊的な実践

これは学ぶべき最初の教訓だ。自分以外の何ものも呪わない、自分以外のなんびとにも責任をなすりつけないと決意せよ。男らしくあれ、立ち上がれ、すべてを自分自身のせいにするのだ。君は、それは常に真実だということに気づくだろう。しっかりせよ。

たった1つの真の義務は、無執着である事と自由

な存在として働く事、すべての働きを神に献げる事である。すべての義務は主のものだ。

どのような人生であろうと失敗ではない。宇宙には失敗というものは存在しない。人は何百回となく自分自身を傷つけ、何千回となく倒れるだろう。だが、最後には自分が神であることを悟るのだ。

ひとつの考えを取り上げよ。その考えを君の命とするのだ、そのことを考えよ、そのことを夢みよ。君の頭脳・筋肉・神経・君の体のあらゆる部分をその考えで一杯にし、他のすべての考えは放っておくのだ。これこそ卓越した精神世界の巨人を輩出する方法だ。

穏やかで、動揺しないほど、良い仕事がなされるだろう。

外側に表れている本性を抑えるのは、望ましいことであり立派なことだ。しかし、内在する本性を抑

えるのはさらに立派なことである。人間の心の内側にある微妙な働きの秘密を理解し、その素晴らしい秘密を熟知して、内なる人間性を抑えるということは完全に宗教に属する。

求めよ、さらば与えられる。探せよ、さらば見つけられる。叩けよ、さらば開けられる。これらのキリストの言葉はでっちあげでも作り話でもなく、文字通り真実である。

君たちの信者仲間を指導しようとしないで、彼らに尽くしなさい。無慈悲な指導熱は、幾多の立派な船を人生の大海に沈めてきたのだ。

行動を起こすのはよい。ただしそれは思考から生まれる。脳をよく働かせよ。高度な思いから最高の理想が生まれる。それを昼も夜も思いつづけることから偉大な働きがなされる。

自己中心主義を止めることが、結局は自分を一番

幸せにすることになる。ただ問題は、人びとにそれを実行するだけの根気がないことだ。

　自分を主に献げ切っている人びとは、すべての、いわゆる活動家よりもよく世のために尽す。自分自身を徹底的に浄化したひとりの人の方が、多数の説教師よりも多くのことを成し遂げる。清らかさと静かさとから、迫力のある言葉は出るのだ。

　自分自身を度外視している時にこそ、われわれは最高の仕事を成し遂げ、最大の影響を与えるものだ。

　実践は絶対に必要だ。君たちが座って毎日１時間私の話を聞いたとしても、実践しなければ一歩も前進しないだろう。すべては実践にかかっている。われわれはこのようなことを自分で経験しなければ理解できない。自分の力でこのようなことを見、感じなければならない。説明や理論を聞くだけではだめだ。

Arise Awake

　他者に善をなそうと絶えず努力することによって、われわれは自分自身のことを忘れようとしているのだ。この自己を忘れることこそ、われわれが人生で学ばなければならない、ひとつの大いなる教訓である。人は愚かにも自分で自分を幸せにできると思い、長年にわたって必死に努力する。そしてやっと、本当の幸せは利己主義を断ち切ることにあり、自分以外の何者も自分を幸せにできないことに気づくのだ。

　利己的であることは不道徳であり、利他的であることが道徳だ。

　瞑想は重要だ。瞑想せよ！　瞑想は偉大だ。それは霊的生活――心が瞑想している――への近道だ。それは、日常生活のなかでわれわれが完全に物質でなくなる瞬間――あらゆる問題から解放されて、魂がそれ自身について考えている瞬間だ――魂のこのすばらしい感触。

その他

　おのおのの魂は星であり、すべての星は、かの無限の青空、かの永遠の大空、すなわち主の中にちりばめられているのだ。各自すべての根、実体、真の固体性はそこにある。

　もはや何者も、彼女（インド）に抵抗することはできない。もはやけっして、彼女は眠ろうとはしない。いかなる外部の力も、もう彼女を抑えることはできない。この無限の巨人が、彼女の足で立とうとしているのだから。

　われわれは愚かさゆえに、自分は弱い、自分は不浄だなどと嘆くのだ。

　われわれは神以外のあらゆるものを欲しがる。われわれの普通の願望は外界によって満たされるからである。われわれの要求が物質宇宙の限界内に限られている間は、われわれは一向に神の必要を感じ

ない。

　幾百万が飢えと無知の中で死んでいる間は、彼らに代償を払わせて教育を受けていながら、彼らに一顧も与えぬ連中の一人一人を、私は裏切り者と見る！

　義務がわれわれの病となってしまっている。義務に引っ張り回されてしまっているのだ。義務に捕らえられた人生は惨めなものだ。

　教育とは、頭に詰め込まれ、未消化のまま、生涯そこで騒ぎ回っている情報量を指すのではない。われわれは人生を構築し、人間を育成し、人格を形成する知識の取り入れ方をする必要があるのだ。

　御身、地上の神々——罪びとたちよ。人を罪びとと呼ぶ事が罪なのだ。

　私の理想は実に数語で現わす事ができる。それは

立ち上がれ 目覚めよ

人類に彼らの神性と、それを人生のあらゆる活動に現わす術を説く事である。

人生は自分を抑えつける傾向を持つ環境の下にある人間の、発展であり進歩である。

人生は戦いと幻滅の連続だ。人生の秘密は楽しみにではなく、経験を通して学習することにある。

生と死、善と悪、人知と無知のこの混じり合いは、いわゆるマーヤー、あるいは普遍的現象と呼ばれるものである。君たちは永遠にこの網の内側で幸福を探し求め続け、幾多の悪にも出会うことになろう。悪いことには会わず、良いことだけを経験するなどというのは、子供っぽいたわごとだ。

予言者たちは、類のない存在だったのではない。君たちまたは私と同じような人間だったのだ。彼らは偉大なヨギたちだった。彼らは超越意識を得ていたのである。そして君たちも私も、同じものを得る

Arise Awake

ことができるのだ。一人のひとがかつてその状態に達した、という事実そのものが、それは誰にでもできることだ、ということを証明している。できることだと言うだけでなく、誰でもがついにはその状態に達しなければならないのであり、それが宗教なのである。

　利他的であることはより多くの利益をもたらす。しかし、人びとにはそれをなす忍耐がない。

　おそらく私には、肉体を脱出した方がよい——着古した着物のようにそれを投げすてた方がよい——と思うときが来るだろう。しかし私は、決して働くことはやめない！　世界が、それは神と一つのものである、ということを知るまで、私は到るところで人びとを鼓舞しつづけるであろう！

Messages in English

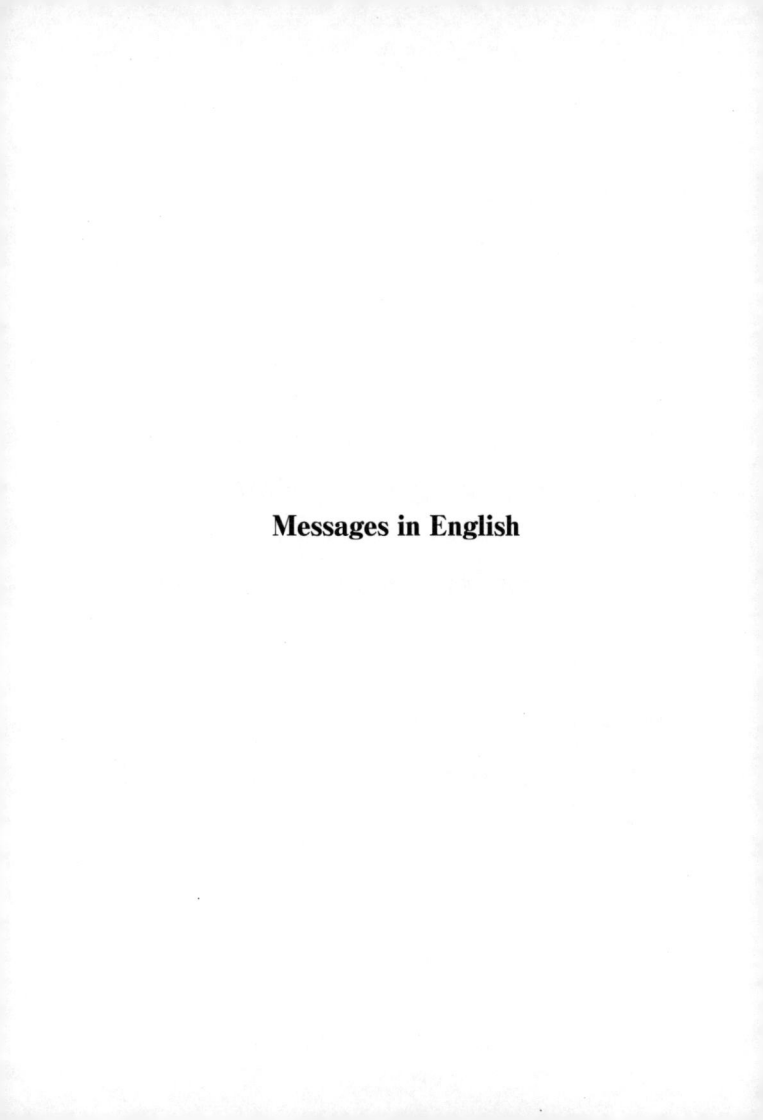

Publisher's Note

This booklet contains some of the inspiring and powerful messages of Swami Vivekananda (Swamiji) – each of which has the potential to transform an ordinary life into an ideal life. The study of these messages and the imbibing of their spirit has impacted many in the past and continues to do so the world over to this very day.

Our sincere hope and prayer is that this book, though small in size, will be found tremendously beneficial to readers even in moments of utter confusion, despair and weakness, and instil in them new hope and power to make their lives worth living anew.

Finally, we would like to mention that Swamiji's messages presented herein do not follow the same sequence in both the Japanese and English segments of this bilingual publication.

Swami Vivekananda
(1863-1902)

Swami Vivekananda, born in India and graduated from The University of Calcutta, came in contact with Sri Ramakrishna, the God-man of Modern India, who became friend, philosopher and guide of his life. Later Swamiji renounced his hearth and home to become an all renouncing monk to realize the highest Truth and to dedicate his life to the service of humanity and attained highest spiritual realisation.

Swamiji became a celebrity in the West as a result of his address on the harmony of religions at the first Parliament of Religions held in Chicago in 1893. He went on to inspire many souls, both in the West and India, with his elevating discourses on Vedanta and Universalism. Many great contemporary and later day Indians including Mahatma Gandhi, the poet Rabindranath Tagore, the statesman Jawaharlal Nehru also drew inspiration from Swami Vivekananda. Some illustrious Westerners were also influenced by Swamiji, for example, Nicola

Tesla, the famous scientist and John D. Rockefeller, philanthropist of U.S.A., Leo Tolstoy, the great savant of Russia and Romain Rolland, the Nobel laureate of France, who wrote a classic biography of Vivekananda.

Swamiji also has a special association with Japan as he spent nearly three weeks here in July of 1893 on his way to the momentous Chicago Parliament and visited Kobe, Osaka, Kyoto, Tokyo and Yokohama. During this visit he praised what he observed were sterling qualities of the Japanese, such as love of country, hard work ethic and aesthetic sense. These praises are noted in a letter written from Yokohama on 13 July.

We know that famous Japanese art historian, Okakura Tenshin, was introduced to the works of Vivekananda through a visiting art student, Josephine MacLeod, a devoted disciple of Swamiji. Okakura later visited the new Ramakrishna Math and Mission headquarters near Calcutta and urged Vivekananda to revisit Japan. Similar invitation also came to him from the celebrated Meiji Emperor Mutsuhito. However, Swamiji's poor health would not allow him to accept these invitations.

That Swami Vivekananda's messages are relevant even today is evidenced by the fact that celebrated thinkers, religious leaders and statesmen still quote them and also innumerable people over the world get inspiration from them.

Messages

Strength and Faith

Arise! Awake! And stop not till the goal is reached.

All the powers in the universe are already ours. It is we who have put our hands before our eyes, and cry that it is dark. Know that there is no darkness around us. Take the hands away and there is the light which was from the beginning. Darkness never existed, weakness never existed. We who are fools cry that we are weak; we who are fools cry that we are impure.

Do you know how much energy, how many powers, how many forces, are still lurking behind that frame of yours? What scientist has known all that is in man? Millions of years have passed since man first came here, and yet but one infinitesimal part of his powers has been manifested. Therefore, you must not say that you are weak. How do you know what possibilities lie behind that degradation on the surface? You know but little of that which is within you. For behind you is the ocean of infinite power and blessedness.

Faith, faith, faith in ourselves, faith in God – this is the secret of greatness. If you have faith in the three hundred and thirty millions of your mythological gods, and in all the gods which foreigners have introduced into your midst, and still have no faith in yourselves, there is no salvation for you. Have faith in yourselves and stand upon that faith and be strong.

First of all, our young men must be strong. Religion will come afterwards. Be strong, my young friends; that is my advice to you. You will be nearer to heaven through football than through the study of the Gita. These are bold words, but I have to say them, for I love you. I know where the shoe pinches, I have gained a little experience. You will understand the Gita better with your biceps, your muscles, a little stronger, You will understand the mighty genius of Krishna better with a little of strong blood in you. You will understand the Upanishads better and the glory of the Atman when your body stands firm upon your feet, and you feel yourselves as men.

He is an atheist who does not believe in himself. The old religions said that he was an atheist who did not believe in God. The new religion says that he is an atheist who does not believe in himself.

If matter is powerful, thought is omnipotent. Bring this thought to bear upon your life, fill yourselves with the thought of your almightiness, your majesty and glory. Would to God no superstitions had been put into your head! Would to

God, we had not been surrounded from our birth by all these superstitious influences and paralysing ideas of our weakness and vileness!

If there is one word that you find coming out like a bomb from the Upanishads, bursting like a bombshell upon masses of ignorance, it is the word, fearlessness. And the only religion that ought to be taught is this religion of fearlessness.. Either in this world or in the world of religion, it is true that fear is the sure cause of degradation and sin. It is fear that brings misery, fear that brings death, fear that breeds evil.

Let a man go down as low as possible; there must come a time when out of sheer desperation he will take an upward curve and will learn to have faith in himself. But it is better for us that we should know it from the very first. Why should we have all these bitter experiences in order to gain faith in ourselves?

Let positive, strong, helpful thoughts enter into your brains from very childhood. Lay yourselves open to these thoughts, and not to weakening and paralysing ones.

Look back on yourselves from the state of the amoeba to the human being; who made all that? Your own will. Can you deny then that it is almighty? That which has made you come up so high can make you go higher still. What you want is character, strengthening of the will.

Make your nerves strong. What we want is muscles of iron and nerves of steel. We have wept long enough. No more weeping, but stand on your feet and be men.

Never mind failures; they are quite natural, they are the beauty of life – these failures. What would life be without them? It would not be worth having if it were not for struggles. Where would be the poetry of life? Never mind the struggles, the mistakes. I never heard a cow tell a lie, but it is only a cow – never a man. So never mind these failures, these little backslidings; hold the ideal a thousand times and if you fail a thousand times, make the attempt once more.

The ideal of faith in ourselves is of the greatest help to us. If faith in ourselves had been more extensively taught and practised, I am sure a very large portion of the evils and miseries that we have would have vanished.

The remedy for weakness is not brooding over weakness, but thinking of strength. Teach men of the strength that is already within them.

The world requires a few hundred bold men

and women. Practice that boldness which dares know the Truth, which dares show the Truth in life, which does not quake before death, nay, welcomes death, makes a man know that he is the Spirit, that in the whole universe, nothing can kill him. Then you will be free.

This is the great fact: strength is life, weakness is death. Strength is felicity, life eternal, immortal; weakness is constant strain and misery, weakness is death.

Throughout the history of mankind, if any motive power has been more potent than another in the lives of all great men and women, it is that of faith in themselves. Born with the consciousness that they were to be great, they became great.

To succeed, you must have tremendous perseverance, tremendous will. "I will drink the ocean", says the persevering soul; "At my will mountains will crumble up." Have that sort of energy, that sort of will; work hard, and you will reach the goal.

We can see that all the difference between man and man is owing to the existence and non-existence of faith in himself. Faith in ourselves will do everything. I have experienced it in my own life, and am still doing so; and as I grow older, that faith is becoming stronger and stronger.

You are the Children of God, the sharers of immortal bliss, holy and perfect beings. Ye divinities on earth – sinners? It is a sin to call a man so; it is a standing libel on human nature. Come up, O lions, and shake off the delusion that you are sheep; you are souls immortal, spirits free, blest and eternal ; ye are not matter, ye are not bodies; matter is your servant, not you the servant of matter.

Love and Service

All expansion is life, all contraction is death. All love is expansion, all selfishness is contraction. Love is therefore the only law of life. He who loves lives, he who is selfish is dying. Therefore love for love's sake because it is the only law of life, just as you breathe to live. This is the secret of selfless love, selfless action, and the rest.

Believe in the omnipotent power of love …Have you love? You are omnipotent. Are you perfectly unselfish? If so, you are irresistible. It is character that pays everywhere.

By means of the constant effort to do good to others we are trying to forget ourselves; this forgetfulness of self is the one great lesson we have to learn in life. Man thinks foolishly that he can make himself happy, and after years of struggle finds out at last that true happiness consists in killing selfishness and that no one can make him happy except himself.

Do not try to lead your brethren, but serve them. The brutal mania for leading has sunk many a great ship in the waters of life.

Doing is very good, but that comes from thinking…Fill the brain, therefore, with high thoughts, highest ideals, place them day and night before you; and out of that will come great work.

I do not care for liberation or for devotion; I would rather go to a hundred thousand hells "doing good to others (silently) like the spring" – this is my religion.

If you want to help the world, do not condemn it. Do not weaken it more. For what is sin and what is misery, and what are all these but the results of weakness? The world is made weaker and weaker every day by such teachings.

Love never fails, my son; today or tomorrow or ages after, truth will conquer! Love shall win the victory. Do you love your fellow-men?

Learn that the whole of life is giving; that nature will force you to give. So, give willingly .... You come into life to accumulate. With clenched hands, you want to take. But nature puts a hand on your throat and makes your hands open. Whether you will it or not, you have to give. The moment you say, "I will not", the blow comes; you are hurt. None is there but will be compelled, in the long run, to give up everything.

Our best work is done, our greatest influence is exerted when we are without thought of self.

Self-sacrifice, not self-assertion, is the law of the highest universe.

That which is selfish is immoral and that which is unselfish is moral.

This is the gist of all worship – to be pure and to do good to others. He who sees Shiva in the poor, in the weak, in the diseased, really worships Shiva; and if he sees Shiva only in the image, his worship is but preliminary.

This life is short, the vanities of the world are transient, but they alone live who live for others, the rest are more dead than alive.

Unselfishness is more paying, only people have not the patience to practise it.

God and Religion

And this religion is attained by what we, in India, call Yoga – union. To the worker, it is union between men and the whole of humanity; to the mystic, between his lower and Higher Self; to the lover, union between himself and the God of Love; and to the philosopher, it is the union of all existence. This is what is meant by Yoga.

Each soul is potentially divine. The goal is to manifest this Divinity within, by controlling nature, external and internal. Do this either by work, or worship, or psychic control, or philosophy - by one, or more, or all of these - and be free. This is the whole of religion. Doctrines, or dogmas, or rituals, or books, or temples, or forms, are but secondary details.

God alone lives. The soul alone lives.

Spirituality alone lives. Hold on to that.

I accept all religions that were in the past, and worship with them all; I worship God with every one of them, in whatever form they worship Him. I shall go to the mosque of the Mohammedan; I shall enter the Christian's church and kneel before the crucifix; I shall enter the Buddhistic temple, where I shall take refuge in Buddha and in his Law; I shall go into the forest and sit down in meditation with the Hindu, who is trying to see the light which enlightens the heart of everyone.

I do not believe in a religion or God which cannot wipe the widow's tears or bring a piece of bread to the orphan's mouth.

If there is a God, we must see Him; if there is a soul, we must perceive it; otherwise it is better not to believe. It is better to be an outspoken atheist than a hypocrite.

In life and in death, in happiness and in misery, the Lord is equally present. The whole world is full of the Lord. Open your eyes and see Him.

In worshipping God, we have always been worshipping our own hidden Self.

It is love and love alone that I preach, and I base my teaching on the great Vedantic truth of the sameness and omnipresence of the Soul of the Universe.

No life will be a failure; there is no such thing as failure in the universe. A hundred times man will hurt himself, a thousand times he will tumble, but in the end he will realise that he is God.

Now comes the question: Can religion really

accomplish anything? It can. It brings to man eternal life. It has made man what he is, and will make of this human animal, a God. This is what religion can do. Take religion from human society and what will remain? Nothing but a forest of brutes.

Religion comes with intense self-sacrifice. Desire nothing for yourself. Do all for others. This is to live and move and have your being in God.

Religions of the world have become lifeless mockeries. What the world wants is character. The world is in the need for those whose life is one burning love, selfless. That love will make every word tell like a thunder-bolt.

The embodiment of freedom, the master of nature, is what we call God. You cannot deny Him. No, because you cannot move or live without the idea of freedom.

The various religions that exist in the world, although they differ in the form of worship they take, are really one.

This unselfishness is the test of religion. He who has more of this unselfishness is more spiritual and nearer to Shiva… And if a man is selfish, even though he has visited all the temples, seen all the places of pilgrimage …. he is still further off from Shiva.

Those who give themselves up to the Lord do more for the world than all the so-called workers. One man who has purified himself thoroughly, accomplishes more than a regiment of preachers. Out of purity and silence comes the word of power.

Through the terrors of evil, say - my God, my love! Through the pangs of death, say - my God, my love! Through all the evils under the sun, say - my God, my love! Thou art here, I see Thee. Thou art with me, I feel Thee, I am Thine, take me. I am not of the world's but Thine; leave not then me. Do not go for glass beads leaving the mine of diamonds! This life is a great chance. What, seekest thou the pleasures of the world? He is the fountain of all bliss. Seek for the Highest, aim at the Highest, and you shall reach the Highest.

We must be bright and cheerful, long faces do not make religion. Religion should be the most joyful thing in the world, because it is the best.

What we need today is to know that there is a God and that we can see and feel Him here and now.

Where would you go to seek for God; are not all the poor, the miserable, the weak, God? Why not worship them first? Why go to dig a well on the shores of the Ganga?

Worship everything as God - every form is His temple. All else is delusion. Always look within, never without. Such is the God that Vedanta preaches, and such is His worship.

Spiritual Practice

It is good and very grand to conquer external nature, but grander still to conquer our internal nature…This conquering of the inner man, understanding the secrets of the subtle workings that are within the human mind, and knowing its wonderful secrets, belong entirely to religion.

Meditation is the one thing. Meditate! The greatest thing is meditation. It is the nearest approach to spiritual life – the mind meditating. It is the one moment in our daily life that we are not at all material – the soul thinking of itself, free from all matter – this marvelous touch of the soul.

Practice is absolutely necessary. You may sit down and listen to me by the hour every day, but if you do not practise, you will not get one step further. It all depends on practice. We never understand these things until we experience them. We will have to see and feel them for ourselves. Simply listening to explanations and theories will not do.

Religion is not in doctrines, in dogmas, nor in intellectual argumentation; it is being and becoming; it is realisation.

Remember the words of Christ – "Ask, and it shall be granted unto you; seek and ye shall find;

knock and it shall be opened unto you." These words are literally true, not figures, or fiction.

Take up one idea. Make that one idea your life; think of it; dream of it; live on that idea. Let the brain, muscles, nerves, every part of your body be full of that idea, and just leave every other idea alone. This is the way to success, and this is the way great spiritual giants are produced.

There is a vast difference between saying "food, food" and eating it, between saying "water, water" and drinking it. So by merely repeating the words "God, God," we cannot hope to attain realisation. We must strive and practise.

Worship everything as God – every form is His temple. All else is delusion. Always look within, never without. Such is the God that Vedanta preaches, and such is His worship.

Miscellaneous

Education is not the amount of information that is put into your brain and runs riots there, undigested, all your life. We must have life-building, man-making, character-making assimilation of ideas. If you have assimilated five ideas and made them your life and character, you have more education than any man who has got by heart a whole library.

Even idiots may stand up to hear themselves praised, and cowards assume the attitude of the brave when everything is sure to turn out well, but the true hero works in silence. How many Buddhas die before one finds expression!

Even the greatest fool can accomplish a task if it be after his heart. But the intelligent man is he who can convert every work into one that suits his taste. No work is petty.

From all of you I want this that you must discard for ever self-aggrandisement, faction-mongering, and jealousy. You must be all-forbearing like Mother Earth. If you can achieve this, the world will be at your feet.

Life is a series of fights and disillusionments … The secret of life is not enjoyment but education through experience.

There is no chance for the welfare of the world unless the condition of women is improved. It is not possible for a bird to fly on only one wing.

This is the first lesson to learn: be determined not to curse anything outside, not to lay blame upon anyone outside, but be a man, stand up, lay the blame on yourself. You will find, that is always true. Get hold of yourself.

This mixture of life and death, good and evil, knowledge and ignorance is what is called Maya – or the universal phenomenon. You may go on for eternity inside this net seeking for happiness – you find much, and much evil too. To have good and no evil is childish nonsense.

Truth is infinitely more weighty than untruth; so is goodness. If you possess these, they will make their way by sheer gravity.

Three things are necessary to make every man great, every nation great:(i) Conviction of the powers of goodness (ii) Absence of jealousy and superstition (iii) Helping all who are trying to be good and do good.

May I be born again and again and suffer

thousands of miseries, so that I may worship the only God that exists, the only God that I believe in – the sum total of all souls; and above all, my God the wicked, my God the miserable, my God the poor of all races, of all species, is the special object of my worship.

I shall work incessantly until I die; and even after death I shall work for the good of the world.

The End

立ち上がれ 目覚めよ
スワーミー・ヴィヴェーカーナンダのメッセージ

Arise Awake
Messages of Swami Vivekananda

2013 年 06 月 09 日 初版第 1 刷発行
2014 年 05 月 01 日 改訂版第 2 刷発行
2021 年 06 月 21 日 改訂版第 3 刷発行
発行者　日本ヴェーダーンタ協会会長
発行所　日本ヴェーダーンタ協会
　　　　249-0001 神奈川県逗子市久木 4-18-1
　　　　電話　　046-873-0428
　　　　E-mail　info@vedanta.jp
　　　　Website　vedantajp.com
　　　　FAX　　046-873-0592
印刷所　モリモト印刷株式会社

落丁・乱丁の場合は送料当方負担でお取替えいたします。
定価はカバーに表示してあります。

vedantajp.com

©Nippon Vedanta Kyokai 2013-2021　ISBN978-4-931148-54-3
Printed in Japan

スワーミー・ヴィヴェーカーナンダの刊行物
(協会出版物より)

スワーミー・ヴィヴェーカーナンダによる書籍
- カルマ・ヨーガ
- バクティ・ヨーガ
- ギャーナ・ヨーガ
- ラージャ・ヨーガ
- わが師
- シカゴ講話集
- 最高の愛

スワーミー・ヴィヴェーカーナンダに関連する書籍
- スワーミー・ヴィヴェーカーナンダの物語
    (スワーミーの注目すべきできごとと彼の言葉)
- スワーミー・ヴィヴェーカーナンダの生涯
    (スワーミー・ニキラーナンダによって書かれた詳細に書物)
- 立ちあがれ、目覚めよ
    (スワーミージーのメッセージを文庫サイズにまとめた書物)
- 調和の預言者

(スワーミー・テジャサーナンダ著、スワーミージーの比較的短く書かれた生涯と教えの記述をあわせた書物)
・スワーミー・ヴィヴェーカーナンダと日本
　(スワーミー・メーダサーナンダ著、バイリンガル本)
・真実の愛と勇気
　(直弟子たちの生涯が書かれた書物。スワーミージーの生涯も一部掲載)
・霊性の師たちの生涯
　(直弟子たちの生涯が書かれた書物。スワーミージーの生涯も一部掲載)
・インド賢者物語［改訂版］(絵本)
・実践的ヴェーダーンタ［改訂版］
　(ヴェーダーンタの高遠な哲学を実践してわれわれの内なる自己の真の性質を悟る方法を説く)
・スワーミー・ヴィヴェーカーナンダの生涯
　(スワーミー・ニキラーナンダ著)
・霊性の師たちの生涯
　(ラーマクリシュナ、サーラダー・デーヴィーおよび
　　スワーミー・ヴィヴェーカーナンダの伝記集)

日本ヴェーダーンタ協会刊行物
(税込価格)

veantajp/ショップ

書　籍

今日をよく生きる　価格 550 円（A5 変型、54 頁）

パタンジャリ・ヨーガの実践　価格 1650 円（B6, 254 頁, ハードカバー）

ラーマクリシュナの福音　価格 5500 円（Ａ5 判、上製、1324 頁）

輪廻転生とカルマの法則［改訂版］　価格 1100 円（B6 判、188 頁）

インド賢者物語［改訂版］　価格 990 円（B5 判、72 頁、2 色刷り）

実践的ヴェーダーンタ［改訂版］　価格 1100 円（B6 判、196 頁）

霊性の光　価格 1100 円（B6, 200 頁）

ナーラダ・バクティ・スートラ　価格 880 円（B6, 184 頁）

ヴィヴェーカーナンダの物語［改訂版］価格 990 円（B6 判、132 頁）

秘められたインド［改訂版］　価格 1540 円（B6, 442 頁）

ウパニシャッド［改訂版］価格 1650 円（B6, 276 頁）

永遠の伴侶［改訂版］価格 1430 円（B6 判、332 頁）

最高の愛　価格 990 円（B6 判、140 頁）

調和の預言者　価格 1100 円（B6 判、180 頁）

立ち上がれ 目覚めよ　価格 550 円（文庫版、76 頁）

100 の Q&A 価格 990 円（B6 判、100 頁）

永遠の物語　価格 1100 円（B6 判、124 頁）（バイリンガル本）

ラーマクリシュナの福音要約版 上巻　価格 1100 円（文庫判、304 頁）

ラーマクリシュナの福音要約版 下巻［改訂版］　定価 1100 円（文庫判、392 頁）

スワーミー・ヴィヴェーカーナンダと日本　価格 1100 円（B6 判、152 頁）インスパイアリング・メッセージ Vol.1　価格 990 円（文庫版変形、152 頁）

インスパイアリング・メッセージ Vol.2　価格 990 円（文庫版変形、136 頁）

はじめてのヴェーダーンタ　価格 1100 円（B6 判、144 頁）

真実の愛と勇気（ラーマクリシュナの弟子たちの足跡）価格 2090 円（B6 判、424 頁）

シュリーマッド・バーガヴァタム［改訂版］価格 1760 円（B6 判、

306 頁)
(ディスカウント本) ラーマクリシュナの生涯上巻 価格 5390 → 4290 円〔中古本のみ〕(A5 判、772 頁)
(POD 版) ラーマクリシュナの生涯下巻 価格 4950 円 (A5 判、608 頁)
シュリーマッド・バガヴァッド・ギーター　価格 1540 円 (B6 変形、220 頁、ハードカバー)
抜粋ラーマクリシュナの福音　価格 1650 円 (B6 判、436 頁)
最高をめざして　価格 1100 円 (B6 判、244 頁)
カルマ・ヨーガ　価格 1100 円 (新書判、214 頁)
バクティ・ヨーガ　価格 1100 円 (新書判、192 頁)
ギャーナ・ヨーガ　価格 1540 円 (新書判、352 頁)
ラージャ・ヨーガ　価格 1100 円 (新書判、242 頁)
シカゴ講話集　価格 550 円 (文庫判、64 頁)
ラーマクリシュナ僧団の三位一体と理想と活動　価格 990 円 (B6 判、128 頁)
霊性の修行　価格 990 円 (B6 判、168 頁)
瞑想と霊性の生活 1　価格 1100 円 (B6 判、232 頁)
瞑想と霊性の生活 2　価格 1100 円 (B6、240 頁)
瞑想と霊性の生活 3　価格 1100 円 (B6、226 頁)

特別割引 (協会直接注文のみ)

わが師 1100 円→ 770 円 (B6 判、246 頁) ヒンドゥイズム 1100 円→ 770 円 (B6 判、266 頁) 霊性の師たちの生涯 1100 円→ 770 円 (B6 判、301 頁)
神を求めて 880 円→ 616 円 (B6 判、263 頁)
謙虚な心　価格 1210 円→ 990 円 (176 頁、B6)
スワーミー・ヴィヴェーカーナンダの生涯　価格 2090 円→ 1650 円 (A5 判、368 頁)
ホーリー・マザーの福音　価格 2090 円→ 1760 円 (A5 判 320 頁)
ホーリー・マザーの生涯　価格 2090 円→ 1760 円 (A5 判 320 頁)
スワミ・アドブターナンダ　価格 1100 円→ 990 円 (B6 判、190 頁)

ＤＶＤ

ヴィヴェーカーナンダ・バイ・ヴィヴェーカーナンダ (字幕付)

価格 2750 円（127 分）
スワーミー・ヴィヴェーカーナンダ生涯の記録（字幕付）価格 2200 円（54 分）

C D

ガーヤットリー・マントラ 108　価格 1320 円（約 73 分）
シヴァ神のマハームリットゥンジャヤ・マントラ 108　1320 円（約 79 分）
マントラム 2090 円→1650 円（約 66 分）
シュリー・ラーマクリシュナ・アラティ　価格 2200 円（約 60 分）
シヴァ-バジャン（シヴァのマントラと賛歌　価格 2200 円（約 75 分）
こころに咲く花　～やすらぎの信仰歌～　価格 1650 円（約 46 分）
ラヴィ・シャンカール、シタール　価格 2090 円
ハリ・プラサード、フルート　価格 2090 円
ディッヴァ・ギーティ（神聖な歌）１～３　各価格 2200 円（約 60 分）
ディヤーナム（瞑想）　価格 2200 円（77:50 分)
普遍の祈りと讃歌　価格 2200 円（44:58 分）
バガヴァッド・ギーター（全集）価格 5500 円（75:27、67:17、68:00 分）
シュリマッド・バガヴァッド・ギーター（選集）　価格 2420 円（79:06 分）

会　員

協会会員には、雑誌講読を主とする準会員（年間４０００円）と協会の維持を助けてくれる正会員（年間１２０００円またはそれ以上）があります。正・準会員には年６回、奇数月発行の会誌「不滅の言葉」と、催し物のご案内をお送り致します。また協会の物品購入に関して１５％引きとなります。（協会直販のみ）